IT'S TIME TO EAT BANANA SPLITS

It's Time to Eat
BANANA SPLITS

Walter the Educator

Silent King Books
A WhichHead Entertainment Imprint

Copyright © 2024 by Walter the Educator

All rights reserved. No part of this book may be reproduced in any manner whatsoever without written per- mission except in the case of brief quotations embodied in critical articles and reviews.

First Printing, 2024

Disclaimer

This book is a literary work; the story is not about specific persons, locations, situations, and/or circumstances unless mentioned in a historical context. Any resemblance to real persons, locations, situations, and/or circumstances is coincidental. This book is for entertainment and informational purposes only. The author and publisher offer this information without warranties expressed or implied. No matter the grounds, neither the author nor the publisher will be accountable for any losses, injuries, or other damages caused by the reader's use of this book. The use of this book acknowledges an understanding and acceptance of this disclaimer.

It's Time to Eat BANANA SPLITS is a collectible early learning book by Walter the Educator suitable for all ages belonging to Walter the Educator's Time to Eat Book Series. Collect more books at WaltertheEducator.com

USE THE EXTRA SPACE TO TAKE NOTES AND DOCUMENT YOUR MEMORIES

BANANA SPLITS

It's time to eat, oh what a treat,

It's Time to Eat

Banana Splits

A dessert so fun and really sweet.

With bananas yellow, smooth, and fine,

Let's build a split, it's snack time divine!

First comes the scoop, all cold and round,

Ice cream flavors that surely astound.

Chocolate, vanilla, strawberry too,

One, two, three scoops just for you!

Drizzle on syrup, chocolate's the best,

Or maybe caramel for a golden vest.

Don't forget strawberry, red and bright,

Each gooey topping is pure delight.

Now add some whipped cream, a fluffy white cloud,

Make it tall and proud, we're allowed!

Swirl it high with a twirly twist,

A mountain of sweetness, hard to resist.

It's Time to Eat

Banana Splits

Sprinkle on nuts or candies galore,

Bright little bits that make us want more.

Rainbows of sprinkles, shiny and small,

It's a colorful feast for one and all!

Here comes the cherry, red on top,

Plump and juicy, it's the final stop.

Perched like a crown, it gleams and shines,

On our Banana Split, it's all so fine!

Grab your spoon, let's take a bite,

Cool and creamy, a taste just right.

Bananas so soft, ice cream so sweet,

This is a treat that can't be beat.

We giggle and smile as we savor each bite,

This dessert turns day into pure delight.

Friends and family all gather 'round,

Happiness in every joyful sound.

So next time you hear, "It's time to eat!"

Think of Banana Splits, such a treat.

Let's make one together, so grand and neat,

It's Time to Eat

Banana Splits

A dessert adventure that's oh-so-sweet!

Banana Splits are more than a treat,

They bring us together, it's so sweet!

Sharing and laughter, smiles so bright,

A bowl of joy feels just right!

ABOUT THE CREATOR

Walter the Educator is one of the pseudonyms for Walter Anderson. Formally educated in Chemistry, Business, and Education, he is an educator, an author, a diverse entrepreneur, and he is the son of a disabled war veteran. "Walter the Educator" shares his time between educating and creating. He holds interests and owns several creative projects that entertain, enlighten, enhance, and educate, hoping to inspire and motivate you. Follow, find new works, and stay up to date with Walter the Educator™

at WaltertheEducator.com

www.ingramcontent.com/pod-product-compliance
Lightning Source LLC
LaVergne TN
LVHW052010060526
838201LV00059B/3956